SAMSUNG NOTE 20 AND NOTE 20 ULTRA BEGINNER GUIDE

20 TRICKS TO HAVE A SMOOTH USER EXPERIENCE

By John Conton

Copyright ©2020

All rights reserved
This book is for public consumption, any reproduction of
any parts of this book must be done with written
permission from the publisher.

ACKNOWLEDGEMENT

I wish to acknowledge the makers and owners of the device that will be discussed in this guide.

DEDICATION

To my dearest tech geeks all over the world.

INTRODUCTION

Hello to you my name is Dominic, and i know you just got your brand-new Samsung Note 20 series. You probably went through the initial setup process but now you're wondering how you can get the most out of your brand new device. Do not worry, this book in the series was put together all for you, so you can make out the most out of your device.

There are several tweaks and things you must have to do on your device to have that awesome user experience and I will reveal them all here, so lets dig in.

Contents

ABOUT THE SAMSUNG NOTE 20 SERIES

First of all, some basic information about the Samsung NOTE 20 series we are learning about. There are several awesome additions to this latest edition of device from the previous editions, and one of the most pronounced feature in the NOTE 20 is the addition of the Triple camera.

Other new features includes:

1. Upgraded microphone.

2. Quality 12 gigs of RAM across the board.

3. Wi-Fi 6.

4. 128/516GB of storage.

5. Bixby

6. Triple Camera

7. 50x Zoom

8. 5G Technology

PERSONAL REVIEW OF THE NOTE 20

So let me give me my honest review about the NOTE 20. Note that this is **MY** opinion.

So starting with the new triple camera, to be honest its quite a very nice feature, this makes the device a very nice buy for you.

About the microphone quality, this is actually something that could be useful for anyone doing online zoom meetings or for those who want to record podcasts.

For the RAM, I'm glad that Samsung decided to give the NOTE 20 series a massive 12 gigabytes of RAM, since a major focus of the NOTE 20 is now multitasking. So this is one of the biggest advantages compared to the other phablets in the lineup, this will definitely help for productivity work like photo and video editing as well. This makes the functionality of the device quite fast. This will make the device download apps and install games quickly, it will make multitasking easy, and it wont buffer during or video calls of while playing games. And of course, a more efficient processor is good for batteries.

The WiFi 6 is a nice little addition, but it's important to note that it really only makes a difference if your house is set up with the Wi-Fi 6 internet router. So if you don't plan on getting one of these routers any time soon, then it really shouldn't matter to you.

About the increased storage, 128-512 gigs of storage is probably the biggest deal that you'll notice about the NOTE 20. This is quite incredible because this gives you space to store as much as you want on your device.

SECURITY

Get your security right immediately. The best recommended is lock screen fingerprint. There is also the face unlock, you will have to register your face features into the settings to do that. So once you turn on your device, you have to set up your fingerprints, set up your face lock. It's imperative to set up a secure lock because it's very important so that people cant get to steal your phone's content. You might lose your phone or leave it behind carelessly.

- Click Settings
- Click lock screen
- Click on the screen lock type you would want to set up

You would see the swipe or pattern lock type but those or not secure. So I'm going to show you how to set up your face lock and how to set up your fingerprint lock but if for some reason you don't want your lock screen to unlock with your face or unlock with a fingerprint, you can actually toggle those on and off.

I'll just show you actually so if I don't want fingerprints to be a part of my lock screen or you want face on lock on therefore authenticating payment apps or something like that but not your lockscreen, just uncheck that box right there in the settings.

- For the face lock
- Click biometrics and security
- Click face recognition, it'll ask for your pattern or password
- Click the setup button

A camera will pop up where you will put your face, it'll scan your face in about three seconds and then you're good, It's incredibly simple. Having a face lock is very nice and it's just a nice way to bypass your lock screen pretty quickly. I'm just just being honest here, I use it often. I know someone probably argue it's not the most secure thing in the world but it works pretty well and at least it requires the eyes to to be open a google

FACE ID SET UP

Setting up your Face ID is quite simple following these guidelines.

To set up Face ID, You have to then configure these settings if you haven't done so already.

1. Go to your settings.

2. Go to face ID and passcode

3. Enter your Passcode.

4. Tap Face ID.

5. Then go ahead and set up face ID by placing your face in the circle provided and moving your head slowly in a circle.

6. Repeat the head motion until it's complete and click Done.

One good thing about fingerprints lock is that you can set up multiple fingers to be able to unlock the phone. You can have as many convenient fingers as you want to be set up to be able to unlock your device. You can also use your fingerprints lock for your samsung pass and samsung pay.

GOOGLE IS BETTER

The first thing I want to talk about is how we can make Samsung Note 20 and note 20 a bit more googly and no offense to Samsung and Samsung fans.

SET UP CHROME AS DEFAULT BROWSER

The first thing is setting chrome browser as your default instead of the samsung internet app. Most people have their details synced to chrome, so its most advisable to make chrome the default browser so that things will be seamless for you on your new device. The quickest way to do this is:

- Click the settings menu.
- Click on Apps and Notifications.
- Scroll down and click on default apps.
- Click on browser app, the browser app is going to be Samsung internet app.
- Click on the chrome app and its done.

It's as easy as that and of course you know you can do that for anything else if you have a different phone dialer app or assistant app or an SMS app that you would prefer to use other than the default apps, you can change all that but our focus is making chrome browser the default browsing app.

SAMSUNG PASS AND GOOGLE AUTOFILL

Samsung pass and google autofill are just like chrome, everything you have in your Google account is synced up with Google's autofill service and so you have to set it up too. To do this,

- Click settings menu
- Just search for it because you can just get lost in the settings menu, just type in autofill service.
- Click on it when it comes up , it comes with autofill with Samsung Pass.

If you've been using samsung devices for quite some time, you might have your details saved inside your Samsung pass account but if you are coming from another type of device or a Google device, it's easier to just to use Google autofill, that way when you open Twitter for the first time or Instagram or Chrome etc on your account that's saved to that Google account, its is going to be automatically sign in right to those accounts once you open them on your new device.

GETTING FAMILIAR WITH THE GESTURE CONTROL

What is Gesture Control?

The gesture control feature is a nice feature that allows the user to control the iPad and its apps using a few simple finger gestures to perform tasks such as

- Tap
- Swipe
- Scroll
- Touch and Hold
- Zoom

How the Fingers work with Gesture Control

1. You can tap one finger lightly on the screen to wake the device or open an app.

2. You can quickly swipe one finger or two over the screen of your device to move over to the next page or move left or right.

3. You can move one finger up and down the screen of your device to scroll up and down. This is called scrolling.

4. You can use a finger to touch and hold items in an app or in Control Center to check out contents before opening, sort of a preview and perform some quick actions. Also, if you are on the Home screen, you can touch and hold an app icon briefly to open a preview menu screen.

5. You can you the gesture control to zoom in and out

Once you unbox your ipad , the first thing you to should do is get familiar with the **gesture control**. This feature is available in the S10, Its good to note that the gestures are going to be very similar to how they are on the S10 series. So basically, if you swipe down from the top right, you always see that you have the control center right there, if you swipe down from the top middle or the top left or anywhere besides the top right, it will be your Notification Center and you can also see the time and everything right there.

If you swipe up from the bottom and hold that's how you can get into the multitasking mode. You can also see where all your windows are open and you can go ahead and scroll in to see all of your open applications. You can also do that by using four fingers - kind of pinching in – to do so.

For the multitasking, if you go into an application like Facebook, and you wanted to have another application side by side and do multitasking, all you have to do is to swipe up from the bottom to bring up the dock and then you can use both applications at the same time side by side. For you to get home, just swipe up from the bottom - you can also use the four fingers as well- to get home.

Lastly about the gesture feature, the last gesture I want to teach you is how to get in and out of applications quickly. How to do this is by swiping on the bottom bar so you can get in and out of applications very quickly. By swiping on the home bar down at the bottom of your iPad is the quickest way to do weave in and out of applications seamlessly. This is probably the most used gesture besides just going home on my NOTE 20, so this is definitely a function that you're going to want to get familiar with and use it a lot because it makes everything very quick, it makes you be able to basically fly through the phone you can get in and out of applications just very quickly.

I hope I made this clear enough and you understood it.

TAKING ADVANTAGE OF THE RAM

The device has a monster 12 GB RAM and runs on a whooping 4500 mAh power battery, so it will be a disservice to you if you don't get the maximum value for your phone with all the high-end specs, so in order to do that just head into the settings of your device.

- Click settings
- Click battery
- Scroll to the power management button and click
- Scroll to the power management and the performance power mode button, this is where you will see the metrcics to optimize and maximize your phone's battery.

The phone out of the box comes with the 60Hz default option which says ''get the recommended balance of performance and battery life'', this is just a modest recommendation by the manufacturers in my opinion, but personally i wont take this recommendation, not when I have a 5000mAh battery and i want a 120Hz refresh rate with full HD,so i have to go for the high performance option. To do this:

- Click Settings
- Click Display
- Click Motion Smoothness
- Select the High refresh rate which is the 120Hz refresh rate.

Its pertinent to note that the 120Hz option is only obtainable at the full HD Plus resolution. And when you're doing this you can toggle this a few things like the brightness and the screen resolution but when you apply some of those options, the screen resolution gets changed, brightness gets changed, the limit CPU gets throttled down to 70%. It would end up messing with your always-on display and reduce the performance of your device, this you don't want so you don't need to touch with your screen brightness or anything. You also don't want any to agitate with your Full HD because you are on a 120 Hertz refresh rate. Just click on the high performance mode, it's going to bump up your CPU speed all the way up to to a hundred percent and it's going to turn off any restrictions for background data.

This simple step is basically going to give you the fastest phone possible and give you value for your money.

THE SQUEEZE NOTIFICATION SOUND

This might sound stupid to you, but I cant really tell the reason samsung developers installed a fart sound notification in this device. Well, many people just think farts are funny, i know that's going to sound ridiculous but anyway I recommend you apply the fart notification sound that comes built-in pre-installed with the note 20 and note 20 Ultra. To do this

- Click Settings
- Click Sounds and Vibration
- Click Notification sound
- Click Fun category. The sound is just called squeeze.

I don't know why it's called squeeze because it's clearly a fart.

So just imagine you're having a tense or awkward conversation with a friend or family member and a notification comes in and boom you've got this farting sound come out, it might just douse the tensed air. I know again this is probably stupid but it's just really funny, lol.

ACTIVATING DOLBY ATMOS

Dolby Atmos is a sound feature technology that enhances the quality of sound on your device whether you are listening via the in-built phone speakers or using headphones, this makes listening to music, watching movies and playing games on your device a wonderful experience. It was introduced in the samsung S9 plus and S10 series.

If you're in the business of having a lot of voice work done with your phone, like you record things or listen to a lot of spoken word like podcasts, then this Dolby Atmos feature is a great news for you because it will make all your voice records sound richer, fuller and more balanced. How to turn on Dolby Atmos ,step by step

- Click on Settings
- Click on Sounds and Vibrations
- Scroll down to Sound quality and effects
- Click on the Sound and effects button
- Toggle next to Dolby Atmos to turn it on.

I definitely recommend yoiu just to go into the sound settings and you can play around with all the system sounds and vibrations to customize them to your taste.

APPS INSTALLATION

There are different type of apps you might need for the efficient functioning of your device. In this age and time, social media apps might top the table of those apps you might want to install from the Apple store.

Social media applications are very vital to modern and today's way of communication with our friends and family, so it's recommended you install social media apps on your device. Depending on your preferred services or the websites or apps you have been using in your previous devices you would have to download these social media apps from the Apple store. Apps like Facebook App, Twitter App, YouTube App, Instagram App, Snapchat App etc. So head over to the Apple Store and start installing these applications on your device.

There are a lot of awesome games you can install too and applications that are just for the iPad, so you should definitely go into the App Store and explore around some of the iPad applications. Once you've installed those applications, go back to your home screen and start organizing them on your home screen.

One application that i would recommend you install is a calculator since there is no calculator built in to the iPad for some reason which we don't know for now. You should definitely install a calculator application.

ORGANIZING YOUR APPS ON YOUR HOME SCREEN

You will have to organize your apps manually one by one to get them to fit to your preferred location you want them to be. It's recommended to pin the apps you would be using more often where they would be very easily accessible to tap on.

So how to do this:

Tap and hold the app you want to move. Then move the app by moving it around on the home screen and then place it where you want it to be. You can also move it down to the dock. A dock allows you to fit a lot of applications down inside of it. If you want to move multiple apps at a time, just go and tap on that while it's in wiggle mode you can see you can move multiple applications at once. This is a nice feature anyways, so just move them around like that, if you can create a folder where you can just put them on top of each other.

You should organize your dock as this is where most of your important applications are going to be. So you have to put all of your most important applications down there. On the right of the dock is going to be your most userd or your recently used applications, you can actually disable this feature if you want to but actually I'd recommend you leave it that way because it does give you access to recently used applications that you may not have in the dock and they may not be as easy to access so.

Like I mentioned earlier, you could just pull an application down from the home screen into the dock and you can move them out the same way as well. However i recommend you should definitely change it from the default look, you can definitely customize it to whatever applications you use the most because once again this is what you're going to be able to get into when you're inside of other applications. If you pull up the dock like that you can get to all these applications without going back to the home screen and by the way if you wanted to disable those recently used applications if it go into settings multitasking in dock you can see down here show suggested in recent apps you could turn that off if you do not want that you also have these other settings you can take a look at as well.

DISPLAY

The masssive 6.9 inch display screen

One thing about this phone is the display screen, it has a massive 6.9 inch HD Plus display that is pushing a ton of pixels, although it is a bit limited when you enable the 120Hz refresh rate.

- Get into the Settings
- Click Display

So there are a few settings inside the display section that you might want to go over. Of course you can choose between light mode and dark mode and that's something you're going to do when you're initially setting up the device but lets talk about the motion smoothness.

MOTION SMOOTHNESS

When you are enabling either the 60Hz at 120Hz refresh rate out of the box, (its nice that this device comes with 120Hz enabled which is great obviously because of the 4000 mAh battery) just know that the processor of the phone is capable to process all the features of the phone comfortable. Having this at the back of your mind means that you're going to want to enjoy this device to the maximum and one of the more key features to enjoy the phone is to enable the motion smoothness so go ahead have that enabled.

BLUE LIGHT FILTER

The blue light filter is nice filter for dark environments, for example when you're in bed or at night sitting on the couch. The good thing about it is that it can automatically sensor the degree of the darkness and adjust, so just have that automatically toggle on via a schedule and you can have it set to sunrise or sunset automatically to which time of the day it is. Another good thing is that it uses the device's location information to make that happen and of course you can just manually toggle it on and off when you want. And you can also do that via the the settings up the scroll as well, so you just have it set on the custom schedule highly recommend you do the same thing also under display.

EDGE SCREEN

Edge screen is a nice feature, there is really no need to talk about edge panels because personally i think the feature is of little importance and just need to go away, but you can enable them if you really want. I'm not here to talk about that because I don't use them personally because they just seem kind of like a waste of space, that's just my opinion.

EDGE LIGHTING

Edge lighting is very cool, so make sure that's toggled on and you can actually customize this really well. So that's the first thing of course you can do about the lighting style but I want to talk about the apps that you can enable for that first. Apps like Hangout get a lot of notifications,others like Snapchat, Gmai, Twitter, Google Voice etc get a lot of notifications too, so these notifications are the things that you would want to have pop up with my edge lighting.

You would want that cool notification effect, and you can get the effects under the lighting style settings. To get here, the steps are

- Click Settings
- Click Display
- Click Edge Screen
- Scroll to lighting style settings.

From here we can actually customize what type of effect we would like, there's a glitter and there is a multicolored glow. Honestly, all these effects look very cool like but then i prefer the nice effect up there at the top of the settings, you can have the glitter with a multicolored go all the way around the display, you can get sort of an echo vibe going on from the sides.

It actually looks pretty sweet as it glows all the way around the side of the device, and you can choose the color you want for this glow. You can also set different colors for different applications, for example you can set red color for your Gmail so you have Gmail notification glow coming in red, you can set green color for Hangouts and you will get the green glow around the phone when you get Hangout notification, you can set more different colors for different apps on our phone so that you can differentiate your phone notifications just by the color of your phone edge glow. I really think that this is awesome.

For the advanced touches, you can customize the

- ➢ Transparency
- ➢ Width
- ➢ Duration of glow

For the transparency and width, you may have that set to high, because you would really want to see the glow. For the duration of the glow, you can change the duration to your taste.

ABOUT YOUR LOCKSCREEN

The lockscreen of your phone says a lot about you, but asides the nice pictures or themes you might want to use for your lockscreen, you would also have to set some things right in this device.

- So Click Settings
- Click Lockscreen
- So from here you can make whatsoever changes you want to.

The first thing I want to go over are the notifications, so out-of-the-box this is somewhat confusing and I was personally very confused by it back in the day. So to get notifications to show up on your lock screen or at least as well as the always-on display, you're going to have to toggle them on by setting button and then this actually gives you a preview of what it's going to look like.

But out of the box its going to be icons only and so instead of having to tap on the setting button or unlock your phone to see what's going on, you may need details and would want to be able to expand those notifications and read them from the lock screen so details.

For the content transparency you don't need a high content transparency and you don't want that to be too low so just try to balance it, I guess it also depends on your wallpaper and what you what you think is aesthetically. Personally, I have mine set to low auto reverse text killer because i use a lot of darkness so i need that white text on the lock screen.

You can also set notifications to make it possible so you can swap between alert and silent notifications or only just alert notifications.

ALWAYS ON DISPLAY

For the always-on-display, scroll all the way down at the bottom of the lockscreen menu.

- So Click Settings
- Click Lockscreen
- Scroll down to the bottom of the settings to the always-on-display button.

You've got to turn on always-on display, to make those notifications to pop up you know every time. Next is the lockscreen notifications make, sure those are enabled and make sure you've got details toggled on, that way you can see exactly what's happening on your device.

One thing about the always-on display feature is that there is a ton of customization about the feature. They are things that you can do inside of there, for example when the screen is off, you can set the blank screen to display to a clock, it will be always on display and you can also customize the clock quite a bit to your taste, you can access all kinds of clock styles right from the clock box.

There is this sort of weird thing that Samsung did in this device, you would notice that the setting for always-on display is not in the section for always-on display. So there at the bottom of the phone you would see the finger print icon.

Personally, I would want that finger print icon to be shown show icon when screen is off, to do this you have to toggle always-on slate app to show never so you can determine when the finger prints is shown. After setting this, you can see that the finger print icon is on the lock screen and you can actually unlock your phone from the lock screen. I don't know why that setting is not under the always-on display settings menu.

SHORTCUTS

So the shortcuts on the lockscreen would be those quick taps on the home screen that you do to take you to apps on your phone without going through the menu.

So you've got a shortcut for camera, shortcut for flashlight, etc you can customize them to suit the most used apps on your phone. Personally, I have to stick with the camera and of course out of the box it comes with the phone, I also stuck with the flashlight so when I'm kind of stumbling around in the dark trying to pick out the house key or so, I can just easily go ahead and flick that open and get my flashlight on.

You can also set any app you want, if you play a lot of blackjack or need Google Drive constantly or maybe you use instagram a lot, you can set any app you want out of there on the lockscreen.

ADVANCED FEATURES IN SETTINGS MENU

The advanced features on this Samsung device are just so exciting, there are three things inside the advanced features that would be discussed, first is the side key

SIDE KEY

The side key has a double press functionality that alows it to open the camera, that's what it is out of the box. When you double click the side key it goes straight to into the camera and this is a very awesome feature.

Being able to get into the camera quickly is very nice and can come in very handy in catching very spontaneous or emergency moments, and of course this works even when the device is shut down or in lockdown mode, you just have to give it that double click and it's going to open up the camera.

LONG PRESS MENU BUTTON

So when you long press the menu bar, the menu wouldn't come up but you would be redirected to this new software power off pop up. This feature is important to use when your phone is not responding properly although this doesn't happen too much in 2020 with these high tech devices, you'd just have to long press and wait for the device of power off. I'm not a huge fan of this, so I would rather press and hold to access the normal power off menu.

SMART POP-UP VIEW

So smart pop-up view works like this, when you get certain notifications, you can have a chat bubble appear on the screen to allow you quickly reply to the message without opening the app. You don't have to dedicate your entire screen to whatever is happening you can just quickly respond to your pop ups.

So let's say you want the smart pop-up view come up so whenever a hangouts notification comes in, first you'll have to turn off the Do Not Disturb. There's also a settings for the pop-up window, from there you can change the transparency or the the opacity of the pop up.

ONE HANDED MODE

This is a large device, 6.9 inches maybe kind of hard to use with one hand especially for children and individuals with small hands. This makes the one handed mode very important. So under one handed mode you will go with the gesture out of the box, it's disabled so you have to enable it out of the box. The gesture is only accessible if you're using system gestures and not the software navigation buttons, you swipe down in the center of the bottom edge of screen, you swipe down right from the middle kind of right where the Samsung pay kind of logo is and boom now you've got your full full access to your device. Everything works as usual, you can do everything you need to do on your phone except that you can do it all with one hand.

It's actually quite beautiful and if you need to get out of the one handed mode, just tap on the blank side of the display screen. And then also if you're left-handed, you can just use that little arrow to get the left thumb access and it's awesome.

G BOARD

I think the Samsung keyboard has gotten a lot better of course it's got swipe functionality and all that but everybody still just likes having G board. With Google's own keyboard you know of course there's different themes you can use for it, you can dive into the settings here

- you can go you can play with themes,
- you can enable/disable glide typing,
- you can change the voice typing settings,
- you can look at the preferences,
- you can set a number row one handed mode height,
- emoji and all the good stuff

so just download download G board from Google Play it's a free download it doesn't cost any money it's just a nice little tip.

CAMERA

Camera section obviously is very important when you're talking about a device such as this. Just dive right into the settings and do these to get the best out of your pictures.

Out of the box, the camera defaults to the 3/4 aspect ratio but that 108 megapixel camera is not enabled by default, so you actually have to go into your aspect ratio setting and then enable 108 megapixel camera. Now keep in mind that picture and video file sizes are going to be much larger than normal when you use that but this actually have good benefits. They pictures come out much clearer and they're really of a benefit if you're printing out your photos. However, I've noticed that the normal camera not the 108 megapixel camera is actually sharper when you zoom in.

SCENE OPTIMIZER

Scene Optimizer is a feature in the camera that automatically use the available lighting in your picture frame/background to adjust the exposure, white balance, contrast and more to get you beautiful pictures, but honestly it doesn't really work effectively. So let's say you're taking a picture of food or taking a picture of shoes and the Scene optimizer makes the phone to manually select the settings of based on lighting of that particular scene. Personally, I wouldn't want that because I want to be in full control of the pictures I'm taking, I don't need bouquet effects automatically applied or anything like that because I can do the editing myself if I want to.

So take that off so that the rear camera is able to choose between different modes and apply them to the best one that suits at any given situation. I'm sure there are people who would rather prefer the phones to do everything for them, that's totally fine anyways.

SWIPE SHUTTER BUTTON

So this is actually awesome, swipe shutter button allows you either create a gif or take a burst shot of people that might want to take a burst shot personally. I love the idea of being able to take a gif of something you know they focus in for you cameras doing its thing as I was saying so you can slide the shutter button or swipe the shutter button towards the towards the edge now to create a gift when you have that applied.

VOICE CONTROL FEATURE

You would also like to use the voice control feature especially in situations like a night shot, or when you are taking pictures in a crowded party and trying to get your friends to adjust for a selfie, you might lose focus in the midst of all this but with the voice control feature you can command the camera to take your pictures without clicking the button.

It's awesome to be able to say certain words like smile or cheese or capture or shoot incase you want a video. This is a very nice feature.

PALM RECOGNITION

Also under the shooting methods you can use the palm recognition if you don't want to say anything at all. If you want to take a selfie, you can just show the phone your palm and you will see the yellow square on the screen that works to recognize your palm.

This is a nice feature to use especially if you have the phone set up on a tripod for your vlog or taking group full pictures.

I hope you take all these tricks into use and get the most out of your device.

ADVANCED SCREEN FEATURES

This section discusses about some advanced screen features and abilities of the NOTE 20 series.

QUICK LAUNCHING

Something really unique to the samsung note 20 and note 20 is that when you move between apps, you'll often find that it refreshes when you reopen it. This is something that you will find that's more common with music apps and creative apps like video editors and I agree that its quite frustrating.

The solution to this is to go to your overview screen, click on the little icon for the app that you're looking in and you can keep it open for quick launching. What it's doing is that it's using all that RAM that's available in ur phone to hold it there so that when you go back to it, it doesn't refresh. This makes so much sense because you have just a lot of RAM on this device, even more than you could utilize maximally (you can go up to 16 gigabytes of RAM depending on what model NOTE 20)

ROTATION LOCK

If you are watching something while you're in bed and you don't want your screen rotating on you all the time, just drop down the notification bar and lock the rotation. As long as you have your rotation lock turned on, the screen wont rotate on you. You can actually choose when you want it to actually rotate, so if you just rotate your phone you'll see an icon show up at the bottom of the screen and once you clicks it your screen rotates for you manually and then likewise for a portrait mode and you click it and it goes back, so keep in mind you have to have your rotation lock turned on.

NOTIFICATION DROP DOWN

If you go to your notification shade and look at the settings often, you will notice every single time you have to swipe down on the notification shade twice in order to get to the quick settings. One way you can make that easy to get right is to it as use two of your fingers not one finger to swipe down.

SPLIT SCREEN MODE

This device has a really big screen and you must want to maximize it when you use it. So if you click your app overview, just click on the app icon up there and then open in split screen view and then you can choose the other app that you want to have to share the screen with it. You can rearrange it however you want and if you want to exit all, just swipe all the way down and that's it.

WINDOWS PIN

- Click Settings
- Type in pin
- Scroll to windows pin and enable it.

This is really a great feature if you happen to have kids or you are letting someone to use your phone to just make a phone call and you don't want them snooping around in your phone.

So if you hit the app overview screen of the app icon there and then you can choose ''pin this app'' and just that phone call app or whichever app or apps you pinned will be left on the phone screen. So if the person tries to exit the app and open any other the app on your phone, the lockscreen will appear.

VIDEO/AUDIO TRANSCRIBER

This is quite mind-blowing, if you're watching a YouTube video or a podcast and you can't really listen to it and you maybe want to read it, all you need to do is to

- press the volume button
- click on the down caret
- you'll see this option that says live caption
- Click on the live caption

What you will see is a box that is transcribing what is happening in the video or the podcast live on your phone natively, you don't have to be connected to the internet for it to work, it's kind of incredible. And if you want to get rid of this live transcribing, you can either go up to the volume button again and turn it off or you just drag it down and turn it off.

PALM SCREENSHOT

Surprisingly not a lot of people know but if you want to take a screenshot, you don't want to do this whole crazy button thing. Get your palm and you just swipe across the screen and takes a screenshot.

NEW SAMSUNG FEATURES

SAMSUNG QUICK SHARE

This is quite innovative because it's a new feature that has started with the note 20 and note 20 Ultra, this is basically just like Apple airdrop just for Samsung phones. You can click an image in your gallery, if you hit the share button there's an option for quick share. Now this works currently just for Samsung devices, so if you have another Samsung device available you can actually send files to the other Samsung from your new device.

DUAL MESSENGER

Dual messenger is quite helpful if you happen to have more than one accounts of a social media service, maybe your personal account and your business accounts or if social media marketing is your thing. Just enable it and you can have multiple telegram/instagram/facebook accounts in your phone and then it allows you to log into all of them simultaenously. It's essentially creating duplicate apps with different logins.

SAMSUNG MUSIC SHARE

There's an option called music share which is really awesome, so essentially what's happening when you have music share on is that you can connect your phone to a Bluetooth speaker, now when you enable music share you're able to have another person connect their phone to your phone that is connected to the speaker. So essentially you're kind of the in-between and you can both control the Bluetooth speaker and the person's phone.

BATTERY AND SCREEN TIME CHART

One important knowledge you have to know about your iPad is getting familiar with the battery and the screen time charts inside of settings. How to do this:

1. Go into settings

2. Go to battery.

Here, this is going to show you a great breakdown of the way your battery life is actually being used. So it's going to show you which applications are using up the most of your battery life. You can get very specific with this by clicking on the bar chart at certain hours and it will show you from 12:00 to 1:00 p.m. You can click on the top chart as well if you want to and it breaks it down by the hour and then of course you can get an average over the last 10 days which is really useful .

Basically, if you click on the show settings, you can see it shows what your most used applications are today and over the last 7 days. It can also show how long you've been using those applications.

END

NOTES

www.ingramcontent.com/pod-product-compliance
Lightning Source LLC
LaVergne TN
LVHW051617050326
832903LV00033B/4542